THIS BOOK
BELONGS TO :

I0829465

COPYRIGHT 2020 DLS EDITION ALL RIGHTS RESERVED AUTHOR, ILLUSTRATOR OR PUBLISHING INFORMATION

ZEBRA

DRAWING N° 01

TURKEY

DRAWING N° 02

SNACK

DRAWING N° 03

RHINO

DRAWING N° 04

RACCOON

DRAWING N° 05

RABBIT

DRAWING N° 06

PINGOUIN

DRAWING N° 07

PARROT

DRAWING N° 08

OWL

DRAWING N° 09

OSTRICH

DRAWING N° 10

MONKEY

DRAWING N° 11

LION

DRAWING N° 12

KROKODIL

DRAWING N° 13

JAGUAR

DRAWING N° 14

HYENA

DRAWING N° 15

HIPPOPOTAMUS

DRAWING N° 16

GIRAFFE

DRAWING N° 17

FLAMINGO

DRAWING N° 18

ELEPHANT
DRAWING N° 19

CHAMELEON

DRAWING N° 20

CAMEL

DRAWING N° 21

BIRD

DRAWING N° 22

WOLF

DRAWING N° 23

FOX

DRAWING N° 24

DEER

DRAWING N° 25

KANGARO

DRAWING N° 26

SEA LION (FEMALE)

DRAWING N° 27

SEA LION (MALE)

DRAWING N° 28

SQUIRREL

DRAWING N° 29

BEAR

DRAWING N° 30

www.ingramcontent.com/pod-product-compliance
Lightning Source LLC
Chambersburg PA
CBHW081631250726
48657CB00009B/2818